The Beatless Album

I0159490

Paul Thomas

www.ebbproductions.co.uk

ISBN : 978-0-9557596-8-0

Dedication

To Grandpa,

for always pushing me to go further.

A quick chat with Paul Thomas

The book you are about to read is the crowning achievement of two to three years work. Setbacks and unforeseen circumstances have resulted in the book being delayed but it is now here.

I wrote the majority of these poems at a time of my life when things weren't the best. Originally I had posted a few of them on a poetry site, without the intention of anyone really reading them. Until my mother had the idea of publishing some of my select favourites with the help of my father, they would have stayed hidden in my phone. To them both I'm truly thankful.

I hope you enjoy your reading of this brief but honest look into my life. I'll see you on the next one.

- Paul Thomas

Contents

Part 1

Genesis

I don't know how to start this.

I guess I'll have to make it short,
Never in a million years would I have thought.
To put a book out there with all my rhymes,
A book with all my jokes, fucked up lyrics and punch lines.

Wow, now I don't know how to continue,
You just signed up to a look into my mind you don't know what
you've gotten yourself into.
Who would of thought that little old me,
Would finally get his voice heard through all the calamity.

What on earth gives me the right,
To pick up a pen and say what I like?
Looks like you're about to see the outcome,
I'd like to introduce you to The Beatless Album.

Night Time Freestyle

I often think about my poems having beats,
Something sweet sounding and soulful with a dab of the streets.
Though I don't know a lot about them I just go by what I'm told,
My mama tried to keep me from there to make sure I'd grow old.
At the time I didn't see the point of her worry,
Now that I'm older I finally understand and wish I could say sorry.
I'm still just young, dumb and naive,
Tryna stay focused so I don't do anything stupid by 19.

M been calling, dropping me hints,
Wondering when I'll realise and finally take the hint.
My 10 year old self would be kicking me now,
Everything he ever wanted I'm turning down, he'd be asking me "how?"
It's funny how what you want at one time so much you don't want anymore,
Why is it we ignore the ones who love us and love the ones who ignore?
Cliché I know but that shit got me thinking,
Whether what I'm doing, I'm doing for the right reasons, man this shit got me drinking.
Stronger than 40 so I don't think of the pain,
Ignoring the fact that she's out there somewhere crying my name.
Never thought I'd have that impact on anyone before,
Now that I have I'm thinking what was I wishing for?

These night time thoughts got me deep in my feelings,
Hoping for the year to be over so I can move past all these dodgy dealings.
Thinking that it'll be better tomorrow, thinking it'll be fine,
Pleasing to know that it'll be December in no time.
2016 coming soon I would have never imagined,
Something my 8 year old self could never imagine.
Nor would he of thought that I'd be where I am today,
Seeing how my life turned out he wouldn't have anything pleasant to say.

I always thought my friends had it together,
They knew what they were doing and knew where they going. But I never,
Imagined that just like me they went through the same shit,
They had the same problems and didn't know how to get through it.
We're all getting better and we're all learning to cope,
Knowing that we're all going through it together gives me hope.
It's always better to know that you're not alone,
Knowing there's someone on the other side who will always pick up the phone.

Lately I've been thinking a lot about my mortality,
The fact that to me I see it as the biggest fatality.
Maybe it's just because I feel like I ain't done enough,
I'm only 18 but I know I'll one day shine like a diamond in the rough.
People through time have always wondered how to live forever,
Do something that makes an impression and guess when they'll forget you: never.
And that's not me saying do something stupid or bad,
Do something that changes the world and not some passing fad.
I sometimes ponder on what future generations will think of us,
Our celebrity worshipping culture where we follow the lives of these
foolish, dumb people and in which some put all their trust.

Everybody's left the city to go further and explore,
I'm still sitting at home waiting to finally leave through the front door.
I know my times coming and I'll be ready when it is,
I just hope to God one day everything will be better than this.
So that maybe I'll be able to take care of my mama like she did me,
So that I can take her around the continents and the many seas.
She's been working like a Trojan and she never stops,
Of all the mothers I know she always comes out on top.
Though she may not have time to sit around all day and gossip,

She's her own independent women and has her own money in her pocket.

As the night passes on I let these thoughts run,
Some I put in here that are sad and some that are fun.
I only speak on what I already know,
Best believe you're in for a show.
My goal was to always get my thoughts out of my head,
Before they consumed me and before I forgot what I said.
I always liked that my poems somehow reflected myself,
I got more at the ready, but for now sit back and enjoy yourself,

It's Real.

Trojan

My mumma broke my heart when she told me she was in the red,
That every month her bank account looked half dead,
Can't remember a sentence cutting me so deep,
I just knew I had to get out there be on my feet,
Cos I don't want my mum to be driving home one day,
And start thinking to herself that there's only one true way,
She starts speeding up and then goes through the red.
She goes faster and faster till she reaches the edge,
And there I am next to her while she's lying on her deathbed,
Thinking of the one thing she never forgot to have said
"Be good".
Cos even now knowing she's only one call away,
The thought of knowing that one unfortunate day,
I have to say goodbye to strongest person of all,
The one who was always there and always around to pick me up
when I'd fall,
Never will there be a day when I'm as broken,
Than the day I have to say farewell to my mother the Strongest
Ever Trojan.

Time

Time can be a funny thing.
One minute you're a child who loves to sing and then all of a
sudden you're wearing a ring.
Time can heal and console.
Time can make things fall apart that were once whole.
Every time I pass something that reminds me of my childhood I
stop and reminisce.
When I was 8 I never thought I would become this.
All the things I used to say I would never do.
Now I'm out there behaving and acting the fool.
Time can do things you'd never imagined.
Time can make you see things you'd never imagine.
I always feel like I'm running out of time.
And that before I know it I'll reach the end of my line.
For years and years many have been fascinated by it.
Can it be manipulated? Can it be split?
Something I've found to be very real,
Is that no matter what time can heal.

The Best Girl I Never Deserved

Shit, I guess this is my love song...

Back in the days of prepubescent's,
Back when the only things I was worried about was school lessons.
I was young and dumb I didn't know a lot,
I did a lot of things without giving them a lot of thought.
Now I'm older all I seem to do is sit and reminisce,
When I should be out there making memories with the people I'll miss.
But I sit at home thinking about women I've lost,
Even the ones in the days where there was no real cost.
It was near the end of a very long day,
I was sitting in music finger on my mouth didn't having anything to say.
Then she turned around to me mouthed some words,
I was in shock and my eyes didn't believe what I hadn't just heard.
It seemed like the girl I'd be crushing on for nearly 2 years,
Had turned to me and said "I love you" but one of my biggest fears,
Was that she was only tryna mess me around.
See Ellie was the type of girl that went unnoticed,
She drifted through school kept to herself and focused.
But maybe that's what drew me too her,
She was quiet and I felt like I really knew her.
Monday I found her in the cloak room during the first break of the day,
I asked if there was anything she wanted to say,
She was nervous and scared and started to shy away,
So I looked her in the eyes and told her everything will be okay.
She made a heart gesture with her hands and showed me,
And that's when my heart started beating fast with glee.
We were only young what the fuck did we know about love,
If we tried to tell anyone else we knew we'd be mocked and made fun of.
So we kept it to ourselves and smiled knowing that no one knew,
We were together for a year and everything felt brand new.
But shit started turning bad I would have never imagined,

13

She started getting angry and I was mad cos some things hadn't happened.
I was only young but I wanted to kiss her,
She was focused and school driven she wasn't yet there.
I kissed her once at a party on the forehead but that was it,
Since then everything moved slowly when I wanted it to be quick.
So my friend Edward told me he knew someone who would,
This girl called Jen who up until then I never looked at but I said "good"
One time during Maths she asked to be excused,
I followed her down there and asked if she would and she didn't refuse.
But I was still with Ellie she was my problem,
And the girl I loved so much a year ago our connection had fallen.
She was going off at me at random times I knew it wouldn't last,
Asking to move away from me while we were together in class.
In the end I decided to be with Jen,
My one regret is that me and Ellie never officially came to an end.
One day the news had just spread,
"Paul and Jen are together everybody says"
I was too busy soaking up the attention to wonder how Ellie was feeling,
Must been hard for her for the one guy she likes to leave her without even concealing,
Maybe had I tried harder shit would have made a difference,
But I don't think her feelings towards me would of been any different.
It's been a while since we last spoke,
I reckon if we met up now we'd laugh it off like some joke.
I guess there were still things we both hadn't learned,
Maybe one day we'll meet again, the best girl I never deserved.

1 O'clock In The Library

Heads down, heads down, heads down,
All I can see from left to right is heads down, heads down, not a
sound.
Just the click clack of computer keys,
The slight creak of people bending their knees,
Searching for the book to help them with their degrees,
Searching for the knowledge so they don't get B's.

But why am I here you might ask?
Am I here so I can complete a difficult task?
Or am I here because it's the only place I can focus my head?
Or is it because the thought of failing fills me with dread?

Hell I only started to care how well I did last year,
Before then the only thing that went through my head was sex,
drugs, and beer.
For 16 years my teachers told me that I was no good,
I grew up thinking that they were right cos at the time I never
understood.
That these pill popping, sheet pushers didn't know shit about me,
One teacher once said that when I left the room it filled her with
glee.
Another one had the nerve to try and say that I was a thug,
Now that teachers in jail, outta us whose the real mug?

I know for a fact I got a long way to go,
I've got a lot of grafting to do until I finally blow,
So I can go back to all these teachers who said I would go nowhere,
And tell them what they make in year, I currently wear,
So until I can stroll around with a golden crown,
Back to work, back to the grind, back to my head down.

Violins

Pluck, pluck, goes the string,
She's in front of me crying about my sin,
Pluck, pluck, goes the string,
I look at her only thinking of the plucking of a Violin.

Train Interlude

I'm just sitting here waiting for this train to move,
Had to swerve the ticket inspectors they probably wouldn't of let
me through,
Running late as usual not a surprise to anyone choo choo,
Trains run down and neglected you'd think the council never knew.

Station on station on station,
Best time for me to expand my imagination,
Always thinking, mind always moving as I pass from location to
location,
Writing beatless songs in my notes as I aim to reach my aspiration.

And if is this being read 1000 years down the line, whomever
Is around and questions why I wrote this just ask yourself, whoever
Does anything for anything I'm just a 'boy' with a lot to say,
whenever people ask me what's wrong I usually just say, whatever.

Part 2

2014

60 seconds
60 minutes
24 Hours
7 days
52 Weeks

31536000 seconds
525600 minutes
8760 Hours
365 days
52 weeks

Twenty Fourteen, Twenty Fourteen, Twenty Fourteen,
Lemme introduce,
Twenty Fourteen, Twenty Fourteen, Twenty Fourteen,
you to the,
Twenty Fourteen, Twenty Fourteen, Twenty Fourteen,
Worst Year,
Twenty Fourteen, Twenty Fourteen, Twenty Fourteen,
Of my life,
TWENTY FOURTEEN.

My First Published Poem

"The poem you're about to receive has been left completely untouched and unedited from the moment the writer first wrote it lying on the floor of his bedroom"

Cos I made the mistake of not picking the second choice
I made the mistake of not speaking out with my voice
Cos when it comes down to it, do I wanna be at home
Even though I'm surrounded by my "family" I never felt so alone
Fuck it we all make mistakes everybody does
But does that mean we should suffer because?
What does that say about my "family" if I'd rather just sit outside on my own
Rather be in the cold than hearing my voice uttered in violent undertones
Laughing and laughing at the mear question
"Haha haha, you don't suffer from depression!"
Depression, oppression, put down, put out, be littled
Walking these streets during the day cos the night time is seen as to cold
The thought of having to go back in makes my neck feel like it's in a hold
Hug me, smile at me, try and reassure me its gonna be okay
30 minutes later, the stairs are still dirty, and I start regretting my birth day
"He's shit, he's shit, he's does nothing but chat shit, all hours through out the day & night"
Fuck you, you twats, you don't know jack, leave me at peace until I can take flight
"He's good for nothing, we've wasted so much, sometimes I wish he would just get fucked!!!"
Maybe in 200 years it'll be different maybe I'll finally be appreciated
They don't need me now but will they in the future if I am to be succeeded!

Do I Raise My Hand?

I try to sleep each night but there's too much on my mind,
Resisting the urge to jump out the window and commit suicide.
Because everyday I struggle with my demons on the inside,
Who tell me I should end it all as there seems to be nowhere to hide.
I've just got to 'grin and bear' it as one day it will be fine,
Easy to say when people aren't always saying things about you from behind.
I cut and cut and cut hoping that one will be my last,
But I just wake up on the floor sweating and breathing fast.
Longer, deeper, more painful, more sharp,
Every swift movement is a life destroying art.
Sideways for attention long ways for results,
Guess after you've done them both all you do is jolt.
Lying on the floor staring up at the ceiling,
In the corner of my eye I can see my arm losing feeling.
As gushes and gushes of red pour out like a jug of juice on a hot summer's day,
Wondering if I'll even last that long, hoping I won't I say.
Nothing but blurred red can be seen from all corners of my eyes,
Maybe this time it's finally worked, maybe at last I have not survived.
Survived the war zone of home, the Death Valley of school, the chatter of the children and all there little minions,
There stupid rhymes, foolish little gossip and all there God awful opinions.
Speaking of God can he hear me up there with all he has going on?
Syria in disarray, the government is affray and I expect more attention than his son?
What would they say? What would they say if they knew the real truth about me,
4th time on the bed,
Blood dripping from my hand to my head, close to death,
And just thoughts of only regrets.
Thoughts of all the mistakes and all the pain in which I've had to suffer,

The fact I never was just an ordinary kid I know will haunt me forever!
Always restricted always kept back and the one missing out,
In 20 years time they'll have the memories and all I can do is pout.
"It doesn't matter now. It doesn't matter at this age",
Well guess what things have changed,
They're no longer the same as in your country or age.
What do you know about the 21st century sage?
I sit up all night with tears in my eyes just thinking and thinking nothing else,
Everyday I feel all willpower is going from head to toe in myself.
These nights are the longest, the hardest, the worst,
All I ask is to go to sleep peacefully so to rest my brain of its thirst.
But that's not the case, no that's not the case, because even when my eyes are shut,
The hell in my dreams is just as hellish as my life when I am up.
I yawn all night and I yawn all day but the sleep it just never comes,
And the alarm clock ends the chance of sleep like the sound of very loud gun.
It can't be dealt with no more, no, no more at all, it shall not stand,
It's times like these I must decide when it's time to raise my hand.
Do I raise my hand to hard painful life and all she has to offer?
Or do I raise my hand to kind hearted death who looks more happy than any other?

Days

I don't have good days,
I have sometimes not sad days,
I have sometimes not mad days,
I have sometimes not glad days,
And sometimes not rad days,

I have days where I don't reach my brink,
But at the same time days where I can't live without a drink.

Sometimes I feel like I've lost the plot, lost the scheme,
So I go into by bathroom and stick my head underwater till I feel
like I'm in a dream.

Some may say my rhymes are to extreme,
Yours would be too if you were a suicidal teen,
With no other way to express your anger and hatred,
At a world where you felt like you were not wanted.

I could spit a rhyme that'd make you fall to your knees and cry,
While at the same time questioning your reasons why,
Why a boy like me with so much creativity,
Has so many demons that need to let him be.

Maybe I'm just being to over dramatic,
You would be to if you felt like all people heard out your mouth
was static.

So tell me how high your confidence would be,
If you were constantly told that you could never reach your
dreams,
Or you were the only artistic one in a family full of scientists,
Who picked apart your goals like a vulture at his wildest's.

Maybe I just need to spend some time improving myself,
Before judgement day comes and Satan drags me off to hell to put
me on his shelf.

While all the other members of my family are up in the clouds,
And looking down on me thinking "You've never made us proud"

Sometimes I think it would be easier to take an automatic straight to my brain,
Or take the biggest knife in the store and sever my main vein.

A friend of mine always jokes about jumping off the side of the M25,
But thinking about it there's probably something he's keeping inside.

I always get the most creative when I'm sad and look up at the sky,
Or when I'm walking through my kitchen and catch a glimpse of a knife in the corner of my eye.

I may know why the caged bird sings,
But the chances of me still rising isn't a realistic thing.

I might just sit down and listen to Biggie Smalls,
Talk about his suicidal thoughts and all his pitfalls.

Maybe it's time for me to finally accept,
That my time on this earth no longer needs to be kept.

I don't really know how to end this one,
Except it may involve a bottle of scotch and shotgun.

When I Was Little

When I was little I wanted to be so many things.
I wanted to fly, play football, I wanted to sing.
I wanted to be the first ever boy on Mars.
I wanted to be the first boy to live in the stars.

Then I got older and older and wise.
I started to see people for who they were and there lies.
And I tried to be open, I tried not judge.
I tried to be forgiving and I tried not to hold a grudge.

It was harder than it looked, oh it was.
Harder than when I found out the truth about Santa Clause.
I never thought I'd see something so scary.
I screamed, I cried, I was frozen in fear...when I found out my mum
was the tooth fairy.

Ourselves

Why is it when things are going good they all of a sudden go bad?
Why is it when I get happy I know I have to get sad?
And I sit in my room thinking why can't I have it all?
Who was it that decided all the rules?
Wouldn't the world be better if everything worked?
Wouldn't the world be better if nobody ever got hurt?

Imagine what a world that would be,
A world where we could all be happy and full of glee,
A world where we'd never have to worry,
I world where we could take our time and never have to say sorry.

Have you never stopped and thought why do bad things happen?
Is it so we don't get complacent and spring into action?

I don't like feeling sad,
But it seems that lately more than ever I have.
I don't really know what to do in that sense,
Maybe I should finally do it and jump over that high railing fence.
Fall in to the deep dark ocean below,
And watch in Heaven as my family and friends tears flow.
I wonder if she'd miss me I wonder if she cared,
I think about her a lot and I know she doesn't which I guess isn't
fair.

Look at me talking about fair like there isn't kids out there with no
water,
Where everytime they step out of their house they're in danger of
slaughter.

The people around me spend their time worrying about trivial shit,
If they lived anywhere else their egos would take a hit.
Maybe they'll finally appreciate what they have,
Maybe they finally stop being so moody and start being glad.
"She's talking to my ex, I'm angry I'm annoyed"

"I heard he's been hanging out with her sister, he better learn to avoid"

Maybe I'm just overthinking this simple thing,
I get it from my mother it's my biggest annoyance, my burden, my sin.

I've been thinking a lot about that recently I don't know why,
Maybe I'm just trying fill my head so I don't start to cry.

It's sad that I have these thoughts and it's hard to talk them out,
Because being a man you can never show emotion, never pout.
How can we live in a society so misguided,
Where everything we do is always so divided?

Why can't we just accept each other for who we are?
So people won't have to pretend to be someone they're not to get far,
Far within a group that we all seem let define us,
And in ten years time we wonder why we made all the fuss.

We're young we're still trying to find ourselves,
Instead of letting outside forcing telling us who we are themselves.

I'm a big advocator of being who you are,
Cos if you're not, boy, you ain't gonna go far.

I'm still waiting for the day when we all finally accept,
That our true colours never need to be hidden and kept.

Late Night In November

I've never felt more alone than I do right now and I'll be honest I
don't know really know why.

Why do I feel like this, it's just not fair,
I'm sitting here in bed I can't even smile all I can do is snare.

Just go to the kitchen grab the biggest knife and open up every
vein in my arm.
It'll be the easiest thing to do in the world and it'll be too late to
stop me from harm.
Or I could stick my head in one of the many ovens in the kitchen.
I could put rocks it in my pockets, jump in a lake and just sink to
bottom, kicking.

I always think the world might be better off without me around,
I doubt even my "friends" would come to my funeral even if it was
10 minutes away from town.

I'm sitting here with so many tears in my eyes,
I'm 18 and all I can do is sit and cry.
Cos I'm too bad to go any further in this life,
In my mind I'm saying "I'm going downstairs to grab the knife.
And I'll take it to my wrist and let the blood drain and go cold like
ice,
Watch my eyes give out so all I can see is black like I'm in a middle
of a heist."

I'll sit before I pull the trigger, cut the vein, jump off, dive in, put
my head in the oven and remember,
How I was willing to let it all go on this late night in November.

Bus Interlude

Back of the bus waiting for it to go,
Head down, hood up, nobody can know,
Eyes fixated on the people below,
Walking past so fast like a slideshow.

Stuck in traffic just before my stop,
Back of the bus and all alone at the top,
Eyes focused now on the people in the shop,
Wondering if I had the chance with their lives would I swap?

Almost there, almost close, almost near my home,
Almost near the place where my imagination roams,
Cos when I'm in the right frame then I'm in the zone,
As it's the only time I can distract myself from being alone.

Part 3

Sundays In Sierra Leone

The kids in the streets.
The church choir sings.
The hot heavy heat.
The church bell rings.

The dust in the air.
The water from the well.
The food being prepared.
The rust of the old but never forgotten bullet shell.

A Conversation

Interviewer: "So Paul we've entered the closing stages of the album"
Err yeah we have aha I would know I wrote it...

Interviewer: "Well I'd like to ask you a few questions if you don't mind"
That's why we are here, go right ahead.

Interviewer: "Why did you decide to write this album"
Well I had so many lyrics and poems that I just needed to get out and I felt this was the best way.

Interviewer: "How long did it take you to write the album"
Well, I wrote the first poem in 2014 when I wasn't in the best place and from there I wrote more so about 2 years.
Interviewer: "Terrific, and finally, are you black?"
Erm...what?

Interviewer: "Are you black?"
What kind of question is that-?

Interviewer:"Well, according to a lot of people you're not actually black, you don't act black, you don't talk black, you don't behave black...?"
Listen, what gives you the right to-

Interviewer:"You're not black, you're a bounty, you're an Oreo, you're an ice Choc"
Who do you think you are to judg-

Interviewer:"BOUNTY! BOUNTY! BOUNTY!"

I Am Not Black

I am not black, words that I've heard a lot in my life,
Different variations and different people saying these words that
cut through me like a knife.
So many comments and so many insults that made me feel less
than male,
Sit back with a bottle of Jack and listen to my tale.

I went to school not knowing who I really was,
Allowing people to get into my head used to be one of my biggest
flaws.
I didn't really know how to think for myself,
When I think about it, it makes me sick to my stomach and it
deteriorates my health.
I think back to my first day of school and the first thing I remember
seeing was a sea of white faces,
200 eyes staring at me like I was something basic.
Of course back then I was only 11 and I didn't know much about
racists,
Didn't know people actually criticised others because they had
different faces.
I let the people who didn't even know where my country was
control my identity,
So much so I got embarrassed when my full name got read out in
class cos it sounded differently.
Different to the common names that they were used too,
Made matters worse that every teacher I ever came across
pronounced my name like their mouth was full of glue.
So it got to the point when a new teacher came into class I had to
cut them off,
So I wouldn't have the deal with the jokes about how my name was
so tough.
Too many times I heard people clicking my name (click)
Like every black person they met is somehow the same (click)
Worst thing is that, that's the mentality they all had,
My school had a junior school and the only black boy in there year
seem to act bad.

He seemed to live up to every stereotype of a black man they knew,
He'd sag low, talk slow and generally didn't have a clue.
Worst thing is I didn't know if he was doing this just to try and fit in,
Or whether he was doing this so he wasn't a target for their name calling and sin.
But I guess we have to do what we can to survive,
Pretty bad feeling when that place happens to be the school you spend half your day inside.

I tried to fit in and so I changed who I was,
I started sagging low, talking slow and all because,
I wasn't confident enough to stand up and say that this wasn't me,
I wanted them to like me and compliment me and when they did it filled me with glee,
But what kind of life is that too live?
How are these white boys gonna tell me what being black is?

I am not black because I don't talk like I am,
I used to get told I spoke like a white man.
This was coming from those I was supposed to call my brothers,
From the same people who were told just like me that we needed to look out for one another.
We struggled enough in life without the addition of this,
Telling your own people what 'your' colour really is.

I was sitting in class on dark Friday afternoon,
Next to Dan, K and Deeny at the back of the room.
K and Deeny started reminiscing about Channel U,
"The good old days of music" turning to me as if I knew.
"Never heard of the channel" I replied back,
K almost choked on his drink he was so taken aback.
Deeny started laughing like what I said was absurd,
I just sat there humbled to scared to say a word.
K turned to Dan and asked if he knew what he meant,
Dan replied "my younger days listening to that channel I spent".
K turned back to me and just laughed again,

"How you don't know that channel just confuses my brain,
You're not black, you're only black by name"
Looking at me as if we somehow weren't the same.
Who was it who made all these definitions and rules?
I don't know whose worse, the idiots who made them or the ones
who follow them like sheep following fools.

My friends and I are closer now though it wasn't always like that,
We used to fight, argue and get into many spats.
But what brought us all together now I look back,
Is the fact we were all told that we weren't black.
And though it's hard to admit we all tried to live up to the
stereotype,
Trying to live up these other people's black prototype.
We've all managed to grow together and become more wise,
And just like Maya we will rise.

18 years I've been told different reasons for why I'm not black,
But when I sit and think back,
About how I used to cry because I couldn't hack,
And because my love for my melanin I lacked,
But now I know that I'm back and on track,
And me and friends from the bottom of their negative comments
we will rise and attack,
Because whether I'm 18 or 80 no one on this planet can ever try
and say that,
Till the day I die that I am not black, nigga.

Orpington's Confession

I think everyday of how little time at teen hood I've got left,
I sit at home in my bed with a vodka bottle and just reminisce.
Been a long time since the days of 08,
When I sit on the bus thinking 5 O'clock was really late.

When I used to think that life was just so straight forward,
That life couldn't get complicated or in any way sordid.
That the people I was with I would be with forever,
But lord knows shit changes, people change and whatever.

I've seen some be banged up, locked down, turned around,
Some have left, some have stayed and some don't make a sound.
Not a sound, not a word, they can't anymore,
Dead man tell no tales that's for damn sure.

There were a lot of things they tried to teach you in those walls,
But tryna deal with the loss of someone you cared about is one of
their learning pit falls.
I ain't gotta lie what's the point,
The truth comes out eventually and it always disappoints.

Because you can't take back words that you say,
Yeah I know that's a right old cliché.
But it's cliché for a reason I learnt that the hard way,
Imagine how you'd live with yourself if the last words you'd ever
say to someone was "no one likes you go away".

2 days later we heard the news from the higher grape vine,
An innocent kid in our class had reached the end of his line.
They found him hanging in his room they didn't know why.

Although it was confirmed otherwise only way you get through it is
to lie to yourself that it wasn't your fault.
He never bothered anyone, now he'll never be an adult.
But you learned your lesson and started being more careful.
So you don't make another mistake and have to be very prayerful.

What's left of the ones I used to know way back when?
I used to think that those connections I had would never end.
As I get older I learned to let go,
Didn't wanna see them, I didn't wanna know.

Cos the same people that I was screaming "till the end" with,
Where same people a year later telling my haters where I lived.
I always wanted people to know who I was,
So I did things for attention and not thinking of the cost.

Now when I walk through my hometown and see people staring,
I wonder if they know me for doing something that I thought was
daring.
Went to so many different schools like an inspector,
Moved to so many different classes I was moving from sector to
sector.

Met so many people saw so many faces,
But still when I turned sixteen there were so many empty spaces.
And I had to accept that maybe it was me,
Had visions of grabbing a rope and finding the highest tree.
I'm much better now and these thoughts have become less,
I joke around a lot but a lot of truth is said in jest.

I draw inspiration from rappers but I can't rap like them.
I draw inspiration from actors but I can't act like them.

Spent a lot of time thinking of things I couldn't do,
Spent a lot of time thinking of things I shoulda knew.

Spent to long putting myself down,
Until my mum pointed out that I wore a green, white and blue
crown.
One that my ancestors suffered to give me,
One that my fathers' dad will never get to see.

And all I got do is keep myself away from this life of sin,
So God willing I don't die before I am forgiven.
And I'm still waiting for the day I get it all together,
It may not come for a while but I'll working for it even if it takes
forever.

I feel estranged in the same 4 walls I've been since birth,
Hopefully my own will know that he'll never be alone on this earth.
Thrown into acid hoping I'd find a solution,
Weren't happy that I was more suited for the lyrical revolution.

They're getting better but it will still take time,
So long as by the day's end I'm 'fine'.
And until I'm walking on the red, dressed up in Italian,
And not surrounded by red due to a magnum,
While those that I've left watch and see the outcome,
Thank you for your time till the next one,
The Beatless Album.

www.ingramcontent.com/pod-product-compliance
Lightning Source LLC
Chambersburg PA
CBHW060644030426
42337CB00018B/3442